SECOND EDITION

Storybook 17

The
Trophy Book

by Sue Dickson

Illustrations by Norma Portadino, Jean Hamilton, Chip Neville and Kerstin Upmeyer

Printed in the United States of America

Copyright © 1998 Sue Dickson
International Learning Systems of North America, Inc.
St. Petersburg, FL 33716

ISBN: 1-56704-528-6 (Volume 17)

All rights reserved. No part of this publication may be reproduced or
transmitted in any form or by any means, electronic or mechanical, including
photocopying, recording, taping, or any information storage and retrieval
system, in any language, without written permission from the publisher.

B C D E F G H I J K L M N—CJK—05 04 03 02 01 99 98

Table of Contents

Raceway Step 34

Page

Baseball in Philadelphia

Vocabulary

1. Joseph
2. Ralph
3. phooey
4. dolphins
5. gophers
6. Philadelphia
7. photos
8. photographs
9. autographs
10. alphabet
11. phonics
12. phonograph
13. telephone
14. trophy
15. pharmacy

Story Words

16. cassette
17. player

3

It was a rainy day.

"Phooey !" said Joseph.

"Phooey !" said Ralph.

No ball game today.
Ducks and dolphins like
rain, but not gophers !

No trip to Philadelphia !
No photographs of the
baseball players!

No autographs on the photos. Joseph was sad and mad. Ralph was mad and sad.

7

"Rain, rain, go away!
Ralph and Joseph want to play,
BASEBALL !!"

Mom said, "Do your homework. Write the alphabet."

Learn your Phonics Song.

"Ralph, put the record on the phonograph or put the cassette in your cassette player," said Mom.

The little gophers
worked. They wrote the
alphabet and sang the
Phonics Song.

Then the telephone rang.

"Telephone !" called
Mom. "It is Dad !"

Girls and Boys: Hold this page up to a mirror.
Can you read where Dad works?

"The rain will stop.
I'll close the shop.
We have to go.
Our team's on top!"

12

"Come on ! Let's go !
Hooray ! Hooray !
Our team will win
A trophy today !"

The End

13

Christopher's Trip

Vocabulary

ch=k

1. school
2. Christy Breeze
3. Christmas
4. Christopher
5. Chris
6. christen
7. chords
8. schedule
9. anchor
10. chrome
11. stomach
12. ache
13. chorus

ss=sh

14. mission
15. admission
16. permission
17. discussion

Christopher was going
on vacation. No more
school till after Christmas.
He would have fun !

15

He would go on a ship
with his folks. It was a
big new ship. Chris and
Dad saw Mom christen it.

Chris said, "Most ships have girls' names, but I like them anyway."

Then the band struck up the chords of The Star-Spangled Banner. Chris stood at attention and sang.

18

Then there was a big party. There were lots of Christmas cookies. Chris had a good time.

19

Start the engines !
Full power !
We're set to sail !

Soon Captain Hank shouted, "Is everyone ready ? We must leave on schedule. The tide is going out."

Rumble rumble went the big engines !

Up came the big anchor.

Toot toot went the big whistle. Out into the harbor went the Christy Breeze. It went out into the sea right on schedule.

There were many things
to do on the ship. There
was even a movie theater
with no admission charge !

There were three dining
rooms !   Chris gave
himself a mission. He
would try every one !

First, Chris went to the Snack Bar. It was a fancy place with lots of chrome. Chris had a lemon soda.

Next, Chris played ping pong with his dad. That was fun, but it was a long session. It made Chris thirsty.

Chris had a root beer soda. Then he began to play shuffle board.

The Christy Breeze

On and on sailed the
Christy Breeze over the
big waves in the sea.

28

"I feel funny," said
Chris. "I feel fuzzy and
green. I have a stomach
ache."

Mom put Chris to bed.

Dad got the ship's doctor.

They had a short discussion.

"No more sodas without permission. Take these pills. Soon you will feel fine again."

31

Soon Chris felt fine. He had a perfect Christmas. What a big Christmas tree was on the Christy Breeze!

The children sang in a chorus. They sang Christmas carols. They had a big Christmas wreath.

Captain Hank's present was the best. He let each child come up to the bridge of the ship.

34

Chris had permission to steer the Christy Breeze and wear the captain's hat! What a Christmas it was!

The End

Brave Heart

Vocabulary

1. heart
2. creatures
3. ocean
4. shoes
5. any
6. very
7. many
8. sure
9. picture
10. once
11. busy
12. come

13. sugar
14. Wednesday
15. live
16. knows
17. early
18. two
19. why
20. from
21. again
22. answer
23. does
24. friend

Brave Heart is an Indian boy. He lives near the ocean.

When he walks in the forest his shoes don't make any noise.

38

Brave Heart is very clever.
He does many good things.

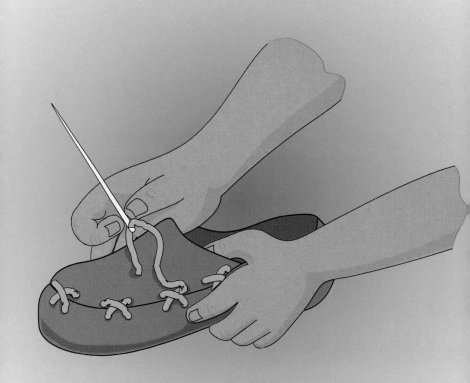

Brave Heart can make his
own shoes. They are very
soft shoes. They are made
of leather.

Brave Heart wants to know many things.

He is learning which
berries are good medicine
and which are not. He is
learning which birds sing
and which do not.

How many living things other than plants do you see in this picture?

Answer: There are eighteen besides Brave Heart.

Brave Heart is sure of all
the paths in the woods.

He likes all the creatures in the woods. There are eleven of them here. Can you find them?

Once on a Wednesday in early spring two deer came to Brave Heart.

"One deer does not look well. Is she sick?" asked Brave Heart. "Maybe she has come to me for help," said Brave Heart to himself.

45

Brave Heart got busy. He
guided the deer to his
friend in the village. The
friend made a strong
medicine from berries and
the roots of plants.

46

The next Wednesday,
Brave Heart said to the big
stag, "I think your mate is
well again."

"Come. We will show
you your reward," the deer
seemed to answer. They led
Brave Heart into the forest.

47

The two deer showed
Brave Heart a big tree. It
was a maple tree. Sap was
dripping from it.

"Mmm, it is sweet. I will
cook some to make maple
syrup. Mmmm! Maple
sugar, too! Thank you!"
said Brave Heart to the deer.

The End 49

Friends

Vocabulary

1. many
2. hearts
3. eyes
4. pizza
5. some
6. soup
7. sure
8. four
9. friends
10. colonel
11. lieutenant
12. sergeants
13. built
14. easy
15. work

Four friends can have fun. They can play together.

Tim, Ed, Sally and Ann are friends. They like to play Secret Spy.

Tim is the biggest. He is going to be the colonel.

Ann will be the lieutenant.

Ed and Sally are to be sergeants.

Ed and Ann helped
build a campsite. Tim
and Sally poured soup
from the thermos. It is
easy if everyone works
together.

53

Ed, Ann, Tim and Sally went on a hike in the woods. They climbed on some rocks. Then they saw some tracks!

54

After that the friends played Secret Spy. Then suddenly they heard many noises! Their hearts began to go "thump thump!"

"Oh, Rex! You sure did fool us! We are so glad it's you!"

Soon it was time to go home.

Tim's dad was at the door. "Where have you been ?" he asked. "Mom has some pizza for your friends. It is hot from the oven !"

"Yippee !"

The End

The Move to Chicago

Vocabulary

1. Charlotte
2. Michelle
3. Cheryl
4. Chalfonte
5. Chicago
6. Chevrolet
7. Michigan
8. Chopin
9. chalet
10. chaise
11. chandelier
12. chef
13. parachute
14. crochet
15. chartreuse

Charlotte, Michelle, and Cheryl Chalfonte are so happy. They are moving to Chicago !

Their chalet home in Michigan has been sold.

Dad will drive the family from Michigan to Chicago in their chartreuse Chevrolet.

The family watched as the movers loaded the van.

In went the chaise lounge.

In went the dining-room chandelier.

In went Dad's chef hat !
In went Michelle's toy
parachute !

"Dad will be our grand chauffeur," Mom teased as they packed the car.

"We will listen to our Chopin music tapes along the way," said Mom.

Soon the moving van was packed and all of the Chalfonte family got into the car.

"I will crochet a new scarf along the way," said Mom.

"Fine, I hope it is for me," said Dad.

Everyone in the Chalfonte family agreed that moving to Chicago from Michigan would be fun.

The End

Have you ever moved? Why don't you write a story about it?

The Enormous Surprise

Vocabulary

1. curious
2. enormous
3. cafeteria
4. yesterday
5. tomorrow
6. fabulous
7. serious
8. explanation
9. detective
10. apartment
11. elevator
12. subtraction
13. together
14. investigation
15. dangerous
16. location
17. generous
18. gorgeous
19. celebrate
20. minute
(minit)

Bob was curious. What was going on in the school cafeteria? Yesterday they had locked the door. No one could come in. Not until tomorrow! What was that fabulous smell? It made Bob hungry.

"I'll go down the street to get my friend, the famous Detective Rick Jones," said Bob to himself. "He lives in the Maple Grove Apartments. He is sure to help me find an explanation."

Bob took the elevator up to the apartment where Rick lived with his mom and dad.

When Bob entered the Jones' apartment, Rick was doing his subtraction homework. Bob told Rick about the "keep out" sign on the door of the school cafeteria.

"Let's go together," said Rick. "This needs an investigation."

71

Finger
Print
Powder

The
Secrets
of
Spying

Detective
Equipment

"Before we go, we need
to gather up my detective
equipment," said Rick.

"All right," said Bob.

Rick and Bob went to the school. They climbed the tree outside the cafeteria window to get a better view.

"It might be dangerous! Be careful!" called Bob.   73

"All I can see is smoke,"
said Rick.

"Wow! What smoke!"
said Bob. "I'll call the fire
department and give our
location!"
74

"What's all the commotion? Call off the fire engines! You boys are too curious! I think I will be generous... come on inside," said the cook.

"What an enormous cake!
It's gorgeous!" cried Bob.

"We can't believe our
eyes!" said Rick.

76

"It is for Mrs.* _____'s class," said the cook. You will know **why** tomorrow."

* Put your teacher's name on the line.

"Yippee ! That's our class !"
yelled Bob and Rick together.
"It's for our year-end Raceway
party."

The next day Rick and
Bob's class had a great
celebration.

"Now boys and girls, you have finished the Raceway Book," the teacher said. "You can read **anything** you want. Isn't that fabulous ? You will each get a trophy ! I have invited all of your parents to join us in the celebration."

Congratulations ! ! !

The End